POPE PIUS XII LIB., ST. JOSEPH COLLEGE
3 2528 01317 1964

Y0-EGD-617

Also by Susan Howe

Poetry

Hinge Picture, Telephone Books, 1974
The Western Borders, Tuumba Press, 1979
Secret History of the Dividing Line, Telephone Books, 1979
Pythagorean Silence, The Montemora Foundation, 1982
Defenestration of Prague, The Kulchur Foundation, 1983
Articulation of Sound Forms in Time, Awede Press, 1987
The Europe of Trusts, Sun & Moon Press, forthcoming
Scattering as Behavior Toward Risk, Wesleyan University Press, forthcoming

Criticism

My Emily Dickinson, North Atlantic Books, 1985

a bibliography of
the king's book
or, eikon basilike

Making the Ghost Walk About Again and Again

On the morning of 30 January 1649, King Charles I of England walked under guard from St. James to Whitehall. At 2 p.m. he stepped from a window of the Banqueting House, out onto the scaffold. He was separated from the large crowd of citizens who had gathered to see his execution by ranks of soldiers so his last speech could only be heard by the attending chaplain and a few others with them on the scaffold.

The King's last word "Remember" was spoken to Bishop Juxon. What Charles meant his chaplain to remember is still a mystery.

Philip Henry witnessed the spectacle. He later wrote: "The blow I saw given; and can truly say with a sad heart, at the instant whereof I remember well, there was such a grone by the Thousands then present as I never heard before and desire I may never hear again."

The gentle and stoic behavior of King Charles I at the scene leading up to his beheading transformed him into a martyr and saint in the eyes of many. His fate was compared to the Crucifixion and his trial to the trial of Jesus by the Romans. Handkerchiefs dipped in his blood were said to bring miracles. On the day of the execution *The Eikon Basilike, The Pourtaicture of His Sacred Majestie in his Solitude and Sufferings*, was published and widely distributed throughout England, despite the best efforts of government censors to get rid of it.

The *Eikon* was supposed to have been written by the King. It consists of essays, explanations, prayers, debates, emblems and justifications of the Royalist cause.

Printers of the *Eikon Basilike* were hunted down and imprisoned. But in spite of many obstacles the little book was set in type time and again. During 1649 fresh editions appeared almost daily and sold out at once. The *Eikon Basilke's* popularity continued throughout the years of the Commonwealth and Cromwell's Protectorate.

The *Eikon Basilike* is a forgery.

At the Restoration, John Gauden, a writer who was also a bishop, claimed authorship. He was advanced to the see of Worcester in recognition of this service to the Crown, because Lord Clarendon and Charles II believed him.

King Charles I was a devoted patron of the arts. He particularly admired Shakespeare. His own performance on that scaffold was worthy of that writer-actor who played the part of the Ghost in *Hamlet.* The real King's last word "Remember" recalls the fictive Ghost-king's admonition to his son. The ghost of a king certainly haunted the Puritans and the years of the Protectorate. Charles I became the ghost of Hamlet's father, Caesar's ghost, Banquo's ghost, the ghost of King Richard II.

In 1649, two months after the execution, John Milton was awarded the secretaryship for foreign tongues to the council of state of the new Commonwealth, in recognition of his pamphlet, *The Tenure of Kings and Magistrates.*

The *Tenure* is a defense of Regicide.

The chief duties of a Latin Secretary were the drafting and translation of international letters and treaties; Latin was the diplomatic language and was used in diplomatic correspondence. While Walter Frost, the general secretary, conducted most general correspondence, Milton was expected to intellectually bolster the new and struggling civil authority. He examined state papers, investigated and interrogated authors and suspected printers, and as a "diligent...partisan, controversialist," composed several crucial political tracts for the Council of State. If Royalists represented the killing of the King, in sermons and pamphlets, as a secular rite of passion; Milton argued that Charles had been an ineffectual leader,

> a deep dissembler, not of his affections onely, by of religion... People that should seek a King, claiming what this Man claimes, would show themselves to be by nature slaves, and arrant beasts; not fitt for that liberty which they cri'd out and bellow'd for, but fitter to be led back again into their own servitude, like a sort of clamouring & fighting brutes, broke loos from their copyholds.

Charles I had been a threat to true Christians who followed their intellectual consciences as informed by God, instead of performing empty and dogmatic church rituals whose purpose was to support a corrupt state. Milton defended a new rationalism in the violent revolutionary struggle.

Eikon Basilike means the Royal Image. *Eikonoklastes* can be translated "Image Smasher."

One of Milton's chief points of attack on the *Eikon* concerned "A prayer in time of Captivity," said to have been delivered to bishop Juxon, by Charles, on the scaffold. The prayer, a close paraphrase from "no serious Book, but the vain amatorious Poem of Sr Philip Sidneys *Arcadia,*" was the prayer of a pagan woman to an all-seeing heathen Deity.

A Captive Shepherdess has entered through a gap in ideology. *"Pammela* in the Countesses *Arcadia,*" confronts the inauthentic literary work with its beginnings in a breach.

Fictive Pamela's religious supplications were a major issue in the ensuing authorship controversy. Scholars and bibliographers accused Milton of "contrivance" in procuring the insertion of her prayer among the King's last devotions in order to ridicule the authenticity of all the gathered notes and essays. The charge has been confirmed, and denied.

In 1680, an official edition of the *Eikon,* sanctioned by King Charles II, subtracted all the prayers. Other post-Restoration *Basilikas* and *Reliquiae Sacrae,* some dedicated to the new monarch, included the seven prayers with Pamela's leading the file. A great deal of energy and confusion has been expended and expounded since then; by bibliographers, scholars, poets, critics, and other impassioned crusaders including Samuel Johnson, Christopher Wordsworth, and William Empson over correctly identifying the first edition to carry the "forged" prayer.

The *Eikon Basilike* is a puzzle. It may be a collection of meditations written by a ghostly king; it may be a forged collection of meditations gathered by a ghost-writer who was a Presbyterian, a bishop, a plagarizer and a forger.

Eikonoklastes is a political tract. It was written by the poet-propagandist-author of "L'Allegro," "Il Penseroso," "Comus" and *Areopagitica, a Speech For the Liberty of Unlicenc'd Printing, To the Parliament of England* while he was acting as the Latin Secretary, a government censor, and an image smasher.

But it is *A Bibliography of the King's Book; or, Eikon Basilike,* by Edward Almack, that interests me. My son found it at one of the sales Sterling Memorial Library sometimes holds to get rid of useless books.

Almack's *Bibliography* was published in 1896 in support of Royal authorship. Francis F. Madan's *A New Bibliography of the Eikon Basilike of King Charles the First, with a note on the authorship* was published in 1950 in support of John Gauden. *A New Bibliography* is still in Sterling Library.

Webster's Third International Dictionary says a bibliographer is "one that writes about or is informed about books, their authorship, format, publication, and similar details." Is he or she supposed to compile a set of authoritative texts that can withstand the charge of forgery, the test of time, the timelessness of libraries?

A bibliography is "the history, identification, or analytical and systematic description or classification of writings or publications considered as material objects." Can we ever really discover *the* original text? Was there ever an original poem? What is a pure text invented by an author? Is such a conception possible? Only by going back to the pre-scriptive level of thought process can "authorial intention" finally be located, and then the material object has become immaterial.

Here is a book called *A Bibliography of the King's Book; or, Eikon Basilike.* Edward Almack meant to describe each material edition, but the vexed question of authorship kept intruding itself.

Pierre Macherey's description of the discourse in a fiction applies to the discourse in this bibliography: "sealed and interminably completed or endlessly beginning again, diffuse and dense, coiled about an absent centre which it can neither conceal or reveal."

The absent center is the ghost of a king.

Oh Lord
o Lord
different from
Laws
zeal
transposed
bearing

OMne
obʍructions
envions
comand

nnfortunate Man
s

un ust
woule
Futnre
audPaged doe of Title-page

Copyright 1989 by Susan Howe

Portions of this book have appeared in The Archive Newsletter *(UCSD),* The Difficulties *and* Temblor.

isbn 0-945926-13-8
isbn 0-945926-14-6 (signed)

This book was funded in part by a grant from the Rhode Island State Council on the Arts.

A Bibliography of
The King's Book
or Eikon Basilike

BY ~~EDWARD ALMACK~~

(MEMBER OF THE BIBLIOGRAPHICAL SOCIETY.)

susan howe

~~LONDON~~
~~BLADES, EAST & BLADES~~
~~23, ABCHURCH LANE, E.C~~
~~1896~~

paradigm press
providence

No further trace

of the printer

IN | HIS | SOLITUDE | To The

Reader the work

Prayers, &c. belonging

to no one without

Reasons

And in a stage play all the people know right wel, that he that playeth the sowdayne is percase a sowter. Yet if one should can so lyttle good, to shewe out of seasonne what acquaintance he hath with him, and calle him by his owne name whyle he standeth in his magestie, one of his tormentors might hap to breake his head, and worthy for marring of the play. And so they said that these matters bee Kynges games, as it were stage playes, and for the most part plaied vpon scafoldes. In which pore men be but ye lokers on. And the; y^t wise be, wil medle no farther. For they that sometyme step vp and playe w^t them, when they cannot play their partes, they disorder the play & do themself no good.

The History of King Richard The Third (unfinished), Sir Thomas More

ΕΙΚΩΝ ΒΑΣΙΛΙΚΗ.

Language of state secrets

The pretended Court
of Justice

Upon the picture of His Majesty sitting in his Chair | before

the High Court of Injustice

Small trespas to misprison

now nonexistent dramatis personae
confront each
other

Heroic Virtue & Fame

Steps between Prison and Grave a Brazen Wall I

Bradshaw went on in a long harangue misapplying Law and History

Thinance
crucified by ordinance
That sea of blood
The malicious author or inswn
Tract the treasons
throw down
Always causes set down
instigator Fort Navy Militia

message
an intellectualist
for a different
of joy
O make me
Some passages
thrown on this person
Was taken
through the populacy
Through populacy
A
piv o t
Contemporary History
The People
In a low voice
two or three words
He bowed down his head and said
He kept
they
pas-

scruples
strive against starry
at times at times

that I hide Security and their
Security

and wall the brazen wall

P r i s o n s

steps between

I am weary of life
Pretend Justice to cover Perjury

The sentiment sentiment
Goes peers ferrets to the last

Obligation

s t e p s

between

P r i s o n s

and wall the brazen wall

that I hide Security and their
Security

I am weary of life
Pretend Justice to cover Perjury

Obligation

The sentiment sentiment
Goes peers ferrets to the last

strive against starry scruples
at times at times

pas-
He kept
they bowed down his head and said
two or three words
in a low voice
The People
Contemporary History

Through populacy
through the populacy
an intellectualist

A
pivot

Was taken
thrown on this person

Some passages

O make me
of joy

for a different message

Always causes set down
gator Fort Navy Militia

The malicious author or insn
Tract the treasons
throw down

crucified by or that sea of blood
That
Finance

ENGELANDTS MEMORIAEL

Tragicum Theatrum Actorum

Similar (not identical)

unsigned portraits of

Laud Charles I Fairfax

Holland Hamilton Capel

Cromwell

Finding the way full of People

Who had placed themselves upon the Theatre

To behold the Tragedy

He desired he might have *Room*

A cleric's forgery
of a pseudo-biographical
apology

to the right
Speech came from his mouth
Historiography of open fields
Signed W King in profile
E
Mend the Printers faults
The place name and field name
as thou doest them espy
Centuries of compulsion and forced holding
For the Author lies in Gaol
All the Civil War Authorities
and knows not why

England's Black Tribunal: Containing The Complete Tryal of King CHARLES the First, by the pretended High Court of Justice in *Westminister*-Hall, begun *Jan.* 20, 1648. Together with His Majesty's Speech on the Scaffold, erected at *Whitehall*-Gate on *Tuesday Jan.* 30, 1648.

An intellectualist out of submissive levelling love

His writings
It passed with the Negative
they kept prisoner
He bowed down his head and said
two or three words
in a low voice
The People
Contemporary History
A
pivot
thrown on this person
Was taken
through the populace
Through populacy
an intellectualist
for a different message
Some passages
O make me
of joy

Dr. *Juxon*. There is but one Stage more, this Stage is turbulent and troublesome, it is a short one; but you may consider, it will soon carry you a very great Way: It will carry you from Earth to Heaven, and there you shall find a great deal of cordial Joy and Comfort.

King. I go from a corruptible to an incorruptible Crown, where no Disturbance can be, no Disturbance in the World.

This still House

An unbeaten way

My self and words

The King kneeling

Old raggs about him

All those apophthegms

Civil and Sacred

torn among fragments

Emblems gold and lead

Must lie outside the house
Side of space I must cross

To write against the Ghost

Bibliography Of The Authorship Controversy

STay Passenger
BE*hold* a Mirror

A First didn't write it

Anguish of the heart
Smart of the cure

Strip furlong field

Feet on someone else's wheat

Easy market access

On-going struggle
abandoned lands

Lost power of expression
Last power of expression

The Battle of Corioli

Obsessive images of Coriolanus

The Author and Finisher
The Author of the Fact

of Gold of Thorn of Glory

Driest facts

of bibliography

Scarce tract work

Load of waste paper

pagination signatures running

The borrower

Stamp of the King's

own character

I am a seeker

Blades Blades & Blades

Tell you my author

I knew his hand

The book was his

The cloathing *Hands*

I am a seeker

of water-marks

in the Antiquity

The Sovereign stile

in another stile

Left scattered in disguise

No men

as expected

ever will be

Saviors

Curtain the background

in the cropping cycle

within the bounds

This word *Remember*

The army and their

abettors

after the murder

of the King

Forever our Solomon

Sent forth into

a Christian world

He is speaking

to the army

Great Caesar's ghost

Through history

this is the counter-plot

and turns our swords in

The First Revolution

The Foundation of hearsay

Horrifying drift errancy

A form and nearby form

In his sister's papers

they often had discourse

The King was trusting

the Kingdom brambles

Printing an edition

of the *Eikon Basilike*

Insertion of prayer

from Sidney's *Arcadia*

The *Eikon* is an imposture

True image antic sun

Amateur such as the King

Saying so I name nobody

Heathen woman

out of heathen legend

in a little scrip

the Firsts own hand

Counterfeit piece

published to undeceive

the world

In his reply Pseudomisus

shifts the balance

of emphasis

Et Chaos & Phlegethon

Mrs Gauden's Nar-/

rative

attributed in Primitive

times to Jesus Christ

his Apostles and other

papers Regicides took

The Dutch Narrative

and Perrinchief's *Life*

Harsnett's *Declaration*

is a weapon

C * R and skull on covers

MADESTIE

More than Conqueror, &c.

Published by Authority

King on the binding

1 blank leaf

The lip of truth

A lying tongue

Great Caesar's ghost

She is the blank page

writing ghost writing

Real author of *The Lie*

"The Lie" itself

fallible unavailable

Thin king the Personator

in his absolute state

Absolutist identity

Imago Regis Caroli

Falconer Madan's copy

the Truth a truth

Dread catchword THE

the king exactly half-face

Face toward the Court Silence

Scope of the body politic
Mock alphabet and map

Daniel's way was to strew ashes
Ashes strewn on his path

Daniel's way Daniel's way
Archaic Arachne Ariadne

She is gone she sends her memory

In the hall Justice Justice
Parable embedded gospel

upheaved among remembrance
Unfinished four last things

Blunt to a wild of nothing
face the Face of the Court

Truth is property and lie theft

Lesser marginal writers

Unutterable gathering darkness
Fragmentary narrative enclaves

Metaphor of a sea raging

Stormy frontispiece

and striking capital D

Threat cord flung

undone in Chalk County

Oak cleft to splinters

storm in the Storm itself

Turned to watch Wrath

Eating our bread heads

we wonder under water

Even after the monarchomachists

The regicide hack

Robert Robin

piled up syllogisms

Opening words of *Patriarcha*

Sentences in characters

Judges and ghostly fathers

The First during his captivity

Omitting the *Life*

almost hissing his regality

off the stage Untruth

SALMASIUS. His Dissection

and confutation

of the diabolical rebel

Milton's book *Eikonoklastes*

So bewitched by him

I am afraid of him

View of magisterial authority
Sound of the hammering

Mask Visor disguised Representer

To walk side by side with
this chapter was Tumult

sacrosanct veils liturgies

First defender of Regicide
Any authority all authority

In Darkness School distinction

of one fact for one fact
What is salvaged saved

exempted that falls Protector

form of figure of thought
Came petitioning to levellers

People under the scaffold

Refusing to be on the scaffold

Vast space where restless
half-forgotten mass migrations

Even the kings of Judah failed

The large cloud breaks open
Style of the Regicide tracts

Fanatical swift-moving authority

Thirsty after fame
in the very Eikonoklastes
he was the author

Impartial Scout
Mercurius Politicus
Melancholicus

suoI
Enakat
r. t e
r e t u a
Per pBruterat

Who is not a wild Enthusiast

in a green medow

furious and fell

Arriving on the stage of history
I saw madness of the world

Stripped of falsification
and corruption

anthems were singing
in Authorem

Father and the Father
by my words will I be justified

Autobiography I saw

Legal righteousness makes us servants
All good hearers

Opposers or despisers
Night page torn word missing

The family silence
gave up the ghost

I feared the fall of my child

resting quietly with some hopes

as a bird before any

This proclamation, beginning 'Charles R. |
Whereas John Milton' is dated Whitehall,
13 August 1660; the text is mostly in
black letter. Milton described as 'late
of Westminster', is said to be in hiding
to avoid trial; the three books are to be
handed in, or else seized and publicly
burnt, and never to be reprinted. The last
line of para. 2 of the text begins 'brought
to Legal Tryal'. This edition is Steele 3239.
with coat of arms, no. 67, measuring $I\frac{15}{16}$ x $I\frac{11}{16}$ in.
And three other copies. Bodl.

Election-Vocation-

Justification-

Cape of wind wreathe

fame out laughing

Seated on cloud

Seacret drift

seacretly behest

the dear She

comes to all Guilty

all circling

Eye window soul body

Pride cannot bow

Ariadne's diadem

zodiac helmet belt

A poet's iconoclasm

A bestiary of the Night

I am at home in my library

I will lie down to sleep

A great happy century

A little space among herds

In the High Quire

We that are distant

Paul also was Romans 7

and Ezekiel 36 I will take away
the stony heart

C

in the ace of speechstone
Spelling surname

Ithuriel

intent

Maii printed so

second i falls below

the line

Maii dropping below

the line

"I Become Friendly With Mr. Dick"

"'Do you recollect the date,' said Mr. Dick, looking earnestly at me, and taking up his pen to note it down, 'when King Charles the First had his head cut off?'

"I said I believed it happened in the year sixteen hundred and forty-nine.

"'Well.' returned Mr. Dick, scratching his ear with his pen, and looking dubiously at me. 'So the books say; but...if it was so long ago, how could the people about him have made that mistake of putting some of the trouble out of *his* head, after it was taken off, into *mine*?'"

He was sequestered pursevanted plundered indgel after sheet 0

Upon authority and extreme rabble [illegible] time of Rebellion

His own peculiar spelling founded on the Scottish prounciation

aftershock of iconoclasm in *Leviathan*   So falls that stately | Cedar

Aftershock of iconoclasm   18th in Wagstaff's first list

utmost
light
mote
Spir e

Therfrom
evry
all edge

Illimited
Ariadne led Theseus
in every
let down
perceptive
Minos' from
daughter
Sphere
Thread
pierced
Thought Trace
weft
Light symbolism
daughter
No
SWADLIER Centuries I
rhid
To her
Face
Fire
CLOATHE
fate
distant
the lay
Island place
deathless
Place they stood on
Stars
away who remember
Flood Crown
she wore
and the sea
Eyes
up
to
Fire

Dominant ideologies drift

Charles I who is "Caesar"

Restless Cromwell who is "Caesar"

Disembodied beyond language

in those copies are copies

K CHARL	WORKS	VOL I
K CHARLE	WORKS	VOL II

Numbers of Prayers, 3.

pp. 1 – 102 ending "FINIS"

It has remains of light blue silk

strings

I was going away, when he directed my attention to the kite.

'What do you think of that for a kite?' he said.

I answered that it was a beautiful one. I should think it must have been as much as seven feet high.

'I made it. We'll go and fly it, you and I,' said Mr. Dick. 'Do you see this?'

He showed me that it was covered with manuscript, very closely and laboriously written; but so plainly, that as I looked along the lines, I thought I saw some allusion to King Charles the First's head again, in one or two places.

'There's plenty of string," said Mr. Dick, 'and when it flies high, it takes the facts a long way. That's my manner of diffusing 'em. I don't know where they may come down. It's according to circumstances, and the wind, and so forth; but I take my chance of that.'

The Personal History of David Copperfield, Charles Dickens

S i lk

symbolic

Praeparative

faith

Ariagne

Idman satter

s e t

the Penned

stars

SUN'S

ARACHNE

deft

ray

through

She shiel

was T sh hr ie ea l dd

winding trace

wool weft

Cloud

soft

threada

twist

paradigm press wishes to thank the following patrons for their generous support:

Kristina Hamm
Donn & Temple Nelson
James & Marlene Frisbie
Victoria & Scott Frisbie
Claudia Fishman
Rachel & Jay Tarses
George Rattner

There are 1,000 copies of this book, fifty of which are signed and numbered by the author. Type used for the cover and the title page was hand set by Rosmarie Waldrop. The book was printed at Thomson-Shore, Dexter, Michigan.